DANDELIONS AND ROSES

MANU

When we are born, we have freedom and courage - like a dandelion that can fly anywhere it wants. But as we grow, everything changes; it becomes hard to accept some things that happen in life. We tend to give up on the things that hit us straight in the face. I was called names like a cynic, psyche, maniac, shit-head and more. Still, I grew up with them due to my decisions, choices and people, but some experiences and people change everything you imagined it to be - like a rose blooming out beautifully from its thorns. That's who you are, my beautiful human and this book is for you

Contents

Contents

Contents

Foreword

Just a beginning of the perfect & beautiful chaos...

Acknowledgements

Thanks to everyone who made me feel alive in my perfect and beautiful chaotic world...

1. When She Came To My Home

When my darling came to visit me
I felt a warmth in my heart, you see
As she walked through my door
My soul was filled with more
Than just the love I knew before
Her smile lit up my world
And her touch was so gentle and curled
I couldn't help but feel so blessed
To have her by my side, no less
Her presence filled my home
With laughter, love and happiness, shown
I felt so happy, so complete
With her here, I could not feel defeat
My dear, you are my light
And in your arms, everything feels just right
I am so grateful for your love
And the joy you bring from up above
I thank the stars above
For bringing you into my life, my dove
I am so happy when you come to me

And I hope that you will always be
The one who makes me feel so free
And fills my world with so much glee.

2. The Two Sides of a Coin Are 

Once he thought they were his kin
But now he feels alone, adrift
Betrayed by friends he thought true
His heart now torn, feeling so blue
He trusted them with all his soul
But they turned on him, let him go
Left to face the world alone
Feeling used, like he's not known
They promised him friendship till the end
But now he's left to fend
For himself, in this cruel world
His trust shattered, his heart unfurled
But still he stands, with head held high
Determined not to let them see him cry
He'll find new friends, who will be true
And leave behind the ones who betrayed him, so blue.

3. When Heart Is Heavy Silence Speaks

A boy with a heavy heart
Thoughts too deep to impart
Silence speaks louder than words
In this pain he is submerged
His mind is a raging storm
Tearing him apart
He longs to let go
But the burden is too heavy to bear
He feels lost and alone
In this darkness he roams
Yearning for release
From the weight of these emotions
His heart cries out
But the silence remains
A suffocating weight
Dragging him down
He longs to be heard
To have someone understand
But the silence prevails
And he is left to bear it alone

MANU

Though his heart may ache
And the tears may fall
He knows that in the silence
He is not alone at all
For in the quiet moments
He finds a sense of peace
And though his thoughts may be unspoken
The silence speaks volumes
about his innermost release.

4. Inner Remorse

Once a young boy, full of dreams and ambition
A heart filled with hope and a mind on a mission
To do good and be great, to make a mark in life
But as he grew older, inner remorse took a knife
It cut deep into his soul, weighing heavy on his chest
An overwhelming guilt that he could not repress
For the mistakes he made, the words left unspoken
The opportunities missed, the promises broken
His ambition now a faint flicker, buried beneath regret
His past haunting him, he can't seem to forget
His inner turmoil consuming him, he can't escape
The burden of his guilt, it's too much to take
But he fights on, determined to make amends
To find redemption, to start over again
To rise above his remorse and chase his dreams once more
And prove to the world, he is worthy of so much more.

5. Better Than Never Trying At All

Once upon a time,
In a land not far away,
Lived a guy who loved with all his heart,
But failed at love time and time again.
He gave his all,
And gave her everything,
But still she left him,
Leaving him to suffer and to sing.
He tried and tried,
But still he failed,
His heart was broken,
And his spirit paled.
But still he persevered,
And still he gave his all,
Hoping one day,
His love would finally fall.
But alas, it never did,
And he was left alone,
Failing at love,
But still moving on.

So take this as a lesson,
To never give up on love,
For even though you may fail,
It's better than never trying at all.

6. Even Though I Give You All My Love

He gave his heart and soul,
But she took it all and left him whole,
His love was pure and true,
But she chose to bid adieu.
He tried to hold on tight,
But she slipped away in the night.
He poured his heart out on the floor,
But she trampled it and shut the door.
He gave her everything he had,
But she crushed his dreams and left him sad.
He tried to move on and start anew,
But his heart was still aching for you.
He thought he found love once again,
But it was just a fleeting fancy in the end.
He tried to make it work,
But his heart was too fragile, it would just hurt.
He failed in love multiple times,
But he still held on to the hope that one day, he'd find,
The one who would love him truly,
And never leave him feeling blue.

He may have failed in love before,
But he knows that true love is worth fighting for.
He'll keep on trying, he'll never give up,
For he knows that one day, his heart will finally find its cup.

7. All She Told Me Was Bye

She said "bye forever" with tears in her eyes,
The guy stood there, stunned and surprise.
He thought they had a love so strong,
But now it seems it all went wrong.
He thought back to the happy times,
The laughter, the kisses, the silly rhymes.
But now it all seems like a distant memory,
As she walks away, his heart feels empty.
He tries to hold on, to make her stay,
But she's made up her mind, there's no more to say.
He begs and pleads, but she remains firm,
Their love is over, it's time to confirm.
He watches her go, a feeling of loss,
As he stands there, covered in frost.
He thought they were meant to be,
But now it's clear, they're meant to be free.
He'll have to move on, start a new chapter,
But the pain of her goodbye will always linger after.
He'll never forget the love they shared,
But now it's time to move on, and be prepared.

8. Let's Not Dive Into The Deep End

He thought love was worth it all
To take the leap and take the fall
But when he hit the deep end,
He found himself in a downward bend
He thought he knew what love was for
But love had left him bruised and sore
His heart was shattered, torn apart
As he realized he'd been played from the start
He thought he'd found his soulmate,
But love had left him in a state
Of confusion, pain, and fear
As he realized he'd been played, oh dear
He thought he knew what love was worth
But love had left him feeling cursed
His heart was broken, lost, and alone
As he realized he'd been played to the bone
He thought he knew what love was true
But love had left him feeling blue
His heart was shattered, torn, and torn
As he realized he'd been played, oh, how forlorn

MANU

He thought he knew what love was meant
But love had left him feeling spent
His heart was broken, shattered, and done
As he realized he'd been played, oh what a shame, what a shame.

9. Strawberry Skies

When I am with you, my love,
The world seems to light up above,
And the sky turns a rosy hue,
As if we're gazing upon a strawberry stew.
Your touch fills me with warmth and delight,
And I am filled with such joy and might,
That the world around us seems to fade,
And all that matters is the love that we've made.
In your arms, I feel safe and secure,
And all of my fears and doubts are cured,
For when I am with you, my sweet,
I know that our love will never be beat.
So let us gaze upon the strawberry skies,
And revel in the beauty of each other's eyes,
For our love is like a beacon of light,
Guiding us through the darkest of nights.
So let us hold each other tight,
And never let go, my love, not tonight,
For when we are together, the world is right,
And the strawberry skies are our delight.

10. Pink Outside & Blue Inside Because Of I

Pink on the outside, blue on the inside
A confusing mix of colors, a battle within
Pink is a symbol of love, of joy and of care
But inside, the blues take over, a heavy burden to bear
The world may see him smiling, acting like everything's okay
But deep down, he's struggling, unable to find his way
He tries to hide his sadness, to keep up a brave face
But the weight of his emotions is too much to erase
He longs to be free from this battle, to find peace within
But for now, he'll keep pretending, pink on the outside, blue
within.

11. Pink Outside & Blue Inside Because Of You

My heart is a canvas, painted with hues
Once vibrant and alive, now dull and confused
Pink on the outside, but blue on the inside
A war between emotions I can no longer hide
I miss her touch, her smile, her kiss
But she's moved on, and I must persist
Pink was our color, our symbol of love
But now it feels empty, like a glove without a hand
Blue is the color of sadness and despair
But I must push on, and show I don't care
I'll paint over the pink, with a new shade of hue
I'll find happiness again, without her by my side
For now, I'll wear my pink and blue
A reminder of love, and a lesson to pursue.

12. That's How It Goes

Once a man with noble intent
To serve with honesty and dignity
But life has fucked him up
With actions taken in reality
He thought he was doing right
But now he sees the consequences
Of his choices and their weight
On his soul and conscience
His heart aches with regret
For the things he cannot change
He longs to turn back time
And make a different exchange
But it's too late now
He must live with the fallout
Of his mistakes and misdeeds
And the loss of all he fought for
He can only hope and pray
That one day he'll find redemption
And learn from his mistakes
To live a life of true intention.

13. Vulnerable Not Desperate

Once I thought love was just a game
A fleeting moment, a passing flame
But when my heart was shattered and torn
I realized how much I longed to be reborn
With someone by my side, to heal my wounds
To chase away the darkness, and light up my moon
I thought I could face the world on my own
But now I see how much I have grown
In need of your touch, your kiss, your embrace
To fill the void and take me to a better place
I never thought I'd be so vulnerable
But now I see, it's not so terrible
To let someone in, to share my pain
To trust and love, and not be afraid
To open up my heart and let you in
And maybe, just maybe, we can begin
To build a future, a life, a home
Together we can weather any storm
So here I stand, with my heart on my sleeve
Ready to love, ready to believe

MANU

In the power of us, and the magic we make
Together we can overcome any heartache.

14. Just A Facade I Say

He thought she was an open book,
But all along she was a crook.
Her words were sweet and kind,
But deep inside she was unkind.
She showed him love and care,
But it was all just a facade to wear.
Her actions were deceitful and sly,
And he was left feeling so high and dry.
He thought she was his partner in crime,
But she was just biding her time.
Her true colors were hidden well,
And he was left feeling like a fool.
He gave her his heart and soul,
But she tore them apart with her lies and goal.
He thought they had a special bond,
But she was just playing along.
He was so deceived by her openess,
And now he's left feeling so helpless.
He thought he knew her inside and out,
But he was blind to her true colors and doubt.
Now he's left to pick up the pieces,
And try to move on from the deceases.

MANU

He'll never trust her again,
And he'll always remember the pain.

15. What It Is

Once upon a time, I felt so lost
Amidst the chaos and confusion, my soul was tossed
My mind was cluttered, my heart was heavy
But now, I feel so normal, so steady
I took a step back, took a deep breath
And weighed everything that was going on in my life, no more a
mess
I let go of the things that were weighing me down
And embraced the good, the beauty, the profound
Now, I am not without challenges, without fears
But I know I am stronger than my doubts, my tears
I have learned to appreciate the little things
The sunshine on my face, the birds that sing
I am not perfect, I am not invincible
But I am content, I am able
I am alive, and that is all that matters
I am happy, and that is all that matters

16. One In A Million

A true friend is hard to find
But I'm grateful to have one by my side
Through thick and thin, through joy and strife
He's been there for me all my life
In times of hardship, when I felt lost
He was there to pick me up, no matter the cost
With a listening ear and a supportive hand
He helped me stand tall and take a stand
I couldn't have made it without him by my side
His friendship has been a constant guiding light
I thank the stars above for sending him my way
For without him, I don't know where I'd be today
So here's to you, my dear friend
You're one in a million, a treasure to the end
I'm grateful for your friendship and all that you do
I'm blessed to have a friend like you.

17. Some In A Million

18. Balanced

Once broken and shattered,
Now strong and precise,
A man who has risen,
From the ashes of love's demise.
No longer a victim,
Of heartache and pain,
He stands tall and proud,
In the face of love's disdain.
No longer looking back,
At the past that once was,
He moves forward with grace,
And a heart that's now just because.
No longer a prisoner,
Of the love that once bound,
He's free to be himself,
And to love without a sound.
No longer a victim,
Of a love that was lost,
He's now a warrior,
With a heart that's not soft.
With strength and precision,
He now faces the world,

No longer held back,
By the chains of a love unfurled.
A man who has risen,
From the ashes of a broken heart,
He's strong and precise,
And ready for a new start.

19. Going Through Changes

He once was in love,
But now he's alone,
A heart once full,
Now a heart of stone.
His pain, it consumes,
His anger, it grows,
His arrogance, it blooms,
As he tries to cope.
He thought he was strong,
But now he's unsure,
His world, once right,
Now feels so unsure.
He tries to move on,
But the memories linger,
He tries to hide his pain,
But it's clear as a finger.
He thought he could handle,
The breakup, the loss,
But now he's struggling,
With feelings of cost.

He once was happy,
But now he's lost,
A guy who went through changes,
After his love was tossed.

20. Acceptance? That's Hard In This Case

My heart is heavy and my mind is numb,
I cannot believe what I have heard.
The girl I loved, the one I trust,
Has done something unacceptable with my best friend, oh how it
hurts.
How could she do this to me,
To betray my love and our trust,
To give away her body so carelessly,
To someone who is not worthy of her lust.
I feel so lost and so alone,
My heart is breaking, my soul is torn,
I cannot fathom how she could do this,
To me, her loving and devoted one.
I thought she was different, I thought she was true,
But now I see that she was just like all the rest,
A heartless, selfish, and deceitful girl,
Who used me for her own selfish needs.
I am devastated and heartbroken,
My love for her was real and pure,
But now I see that she was not worth it,

And I must move on and find someone who is.
I will not let her actions define me,
Or make me bitter and filled with hate,
I will rise above this pain and heartache,
And find someone who will truly love and appreciate.
For now, I will mourn the loss of her,
And the love that I thought was true,
But I know that better things are in store for me,
And I will find happiness, just not with you.

21. Love Is All He Knew

He knew love was unconditional
From the moment he met her
He gave all of himself
Time, energy, and care
His heart was full and open
Ready to take on the world
With her by his side
He felt like he could conquer anything
He was there for her
Through the good times and the bad
Never once doubting
The love they shared
He showed her what it means
To be truly loved
And in return, she gave him
The same unconditional love
Together they were unstoppable
Their love a force to be reckoned with
Their bond unbreakable
Their love eternal
He knew he was lucky
To have found someone

Who loved him just as he was
Unconditionally, without end.

22. But Has To Taste The Hate As Well

He gave all his love,
Unconditional and true,
Time, energy, and care,
But in the end, he was deceived.
He thought she was the one,
But she was not what she seemed,
She took all he had to give,
And then left him to dream.
He thought he knew her heart,
But it was just a facade,
She played him like a fool,
And left him feeling flawed.
He thought he could trust,
But she proved him wrong,
She cheated and lied,
And now he's all alone.
He thought love was pure,
But she showed him its flaw,
Now he knows the truth,
And he's moving on with a heart so raw.

He thought he could love,
But now he knows the cost,
He gave it his all,
But in the end, it was lost.

23. Sorry

Once I treated her so bad
When she rejected my love
I couldn't believe it then
That she didn't want me enough
I acted out in anger
And said some cruel words
Hurtful and untrue
I regret them now, it's absurd
I didn't mean to hurt her
But my pride got in the way
I thought I was entitled
To her love, every single day
But she had the right
To say no to me
And I should have respected that
But instead, I couldn't see
Now I'm left with guilt
And a heavy heart
I wish I could take it back
And make a fresh start
I'm sorry for the pain
I caused her that day

I hope she can forgive me
And let me make it right, somehow.

24. Which One?

In this game of love, I am lost
Two girls, both of whom have my heart
Each one making me feel so alive
But how can I choose between them, when they are both so right?
One with hair of burgundy and eyes of brown
Her smile lights up my world, like the morning dew
She makes me feel like I'm on top of the world
Her gentle voice and sweet words, leave me in a whirl
The other with hair of black and eyes of brown
Her fiery spirit ignites a passion deep within
She makes me feel alive, like I'm on fire
Her fiery touch and passionate words, leave me in desire
I am torn between these two, my heart in a bind
How can I choose between them, when they both make me feel so
alive?
Each one holding a piece of my heart
But how can I give them both, without tearing myself apart?
I am confused, and lost in this game of love
But one thing is for sure, my heart will never give up
For in the end, I know that true love will find its way
And guide me to the one, who will forever stay.

25. She Is My Compass, I Say

A guiding light, a shining star,
A source of love and comfort near,
A beacon in the darkest night,
A source of warmth and joy so dear.
With her by my side, I am never lost,
Her gentle voice, a soothing balm,
She guides me through the darkest storm,
And helps me find my way back home.
I am so grateful, so full of joy,
To have her by my side, my guide,
She is my rock, my constant friend,
She helps me stay true to the end.
Her love is like a shining light,
That guides me through the darkest night,
And I am so happy, so full of cheer,
To have her by my side, to guide me here.

26. Girl In A Red Saree

In a red saree she came to me
And my heart skipped a beat
Her beauty took my breath away
And I felt so happy to see
The way the fabric draped her curves
And the way it shimmered in the light
I could not take my eyes off her
And I knew that I was in love that night
The color of passion and desire
Suited her perfectly, I could see
And as she danced and twirled for me
I felt my heart sing with glee
In a red saree, she was my queen
And I was her devoted king
Together we danced and laughed and loved
In a moment that felt like a dream
I am grateful for that night
And the way she looked in red
For in that moment, I knew
That our love was meant to be.

27. Girl With Her Nerves

As I sit and watch her work
Her fingers flying across the keys
I can't help but be mesmerized
By the way her nerves come alive
Her neck starts to twitch and writhe
As she talks and laughs with ease
I can't help but feel a little crazy
As I watch her nerves come out to play
Her hands move with such grace and speed
As she types and clicks away
I can't help but feel a little wild
As I watch her nerves dance and sway
She is a force to be reckoned with
Her mind and body working in sync
I can't help but feel a little dazed
As I watch her nerves come alive
But despite my crazy thoughts
I can't help but be drawn to her
For in her nerves I see passion
And in that, I am truly smitten.

28. Girl With Burgundy Hair

Burgundy hair, oh how it shines,
A dazzling color, so unique and fine.
I've never seen such beauty before,
My heart beats fast, I can't ignore.
She moves with grace, a queen of the night,
Her smile so bright, it gives me delight.
I'm lost in her eyes, a deep burgundy hue,
I want to know more, I want to pursue.
Her hair flows like a river of wine,
I'm drawn to her, I can't decline.
I want to touch it, feel it in my hands,
I want to be close, be her biggest fan.
She's like a rose, a bloom in the garden,
A beauty so rare, a treasure hidden.
I'm captivated by her burgundy hair,
I'm falling for her, I can't help but stare.
She's a mystery, a puzzle to solve,
But I'm willing to try, I'll do what it takes.
For a girl with burgundy hair, I'd do anything,
I'm ready to take the plunge, I'll give her my heart's ring.

29. Girl In The Black Dress

In a black midi dress, she looked so fine
Her beauty shone like a beacon divine
He couldn't help but feel so cute
As he gazed upon her in awe, mute
Her curves were on display, oh so neat
He felt his heart skip a beat
Her hair was styled in perfect waves
He felt like he was in a daze
She moved with grace and elegance
He was smitten with her presence
He couldn't take his eyes off her
His heart beat faster, oh so sure
She was the embodiment of perfection
He felt like he was in a dream, an obsession
He was completely mesmerized
By her beauty, he was mesmerized
In that black midi dress, she was a vision
A goddess of beauty and precision
He felt like the luckiest guy alive
As he gazed upon her, he felt so alive.

30. The Thought That I Might Lose You

In the dark of the night
I lay awake, feeling so alone
Thinking of her, the one I love
And how she might be gone
The thought is like a knife
Piercing through my heart
How could she leave me
When we've been inseparable from the start
I try to push the thought away
But it haunts me like a ghost
And as I lay here in the dark
I feel like my world is about to implode
I miss her voice, her laugh, her smile
I miss the way she made me feel
And now I'm left with nothing
But the pain of losing her, so real
I wish I could turn back time
And make things right
But now I'm left with just the night
And the fear that she might not talk to me again, tonight.

31. She Said, "Will You Be My Solider?"

Oh sweet lady, how could I refuse
Your offer to be your solider, so true
I'll stand by your side, through thick and thin
I'll be your rock, your loyal kin
I'll fight for your love, with all my might
I'll defend your heart with all my might
I'll be your shield, in times of war
I'll never let you down, I swear
I'll march by your side, into battle
I'll fight for our love, no matter the rattle
I'll be your solider, till the end
I'll be your protector, until the very end
So sweet lady, I humbly accept
Your offer to be your solider, I'll never neglect
I'll be by your side, through joy and sorrow
I'll be your solider, now and tomorrow.

32. Die For You

In your eyes, I see a love so true
A love that I want to give to you
From the depths of my heart, I'll never stray
I'll give you everything, every single day
I'll be the shoulder you can lean on
I'll be the one to make you strong
I'll hold you close, never let you go
I'll be there for you, through the highs and lows
I'd die for you, my love, that's no lie
I'll do anything to keep you by my side
Your happiness is all I crave
I'll do whatever it takes, to keep you safe
So take my hand, and never let go
Together, we'll face whatever comes our way
I love you now, and forevermore
I'll die for you, my love, I swear.

33. Just A Phase

In this uncertain phase,
My thoughts are jumbled,
A tangled mess,
That I cannot express.
I try to speak,
But the words get stuck,
Trapped inside my head,
Unable to break free.
I feel lost,
Confused,
Unable to navigate,
Through this storm inside.
I want to share,
My feelings, my thoughts,
But they remain locked,
In this uncertainty phase.
I am a prisoner,
Of my own mind,
Unable to escape,
This endless maze.
But I hold on,
To a glimmer of hope,

MANU

That one day,
I'll find my way out.
And when that day comes,
I'll speak my truth,
And finally, express,
The thoughts that were trapped within.

34. I Warned Myself

He warned himself to stay away
From the girl with the bright, shining eyes
But he couldn't resist her charms
And fell in love again
He knew the pain she could bring
But still he couldn't let her go
He knew the heartache that was to come
But still he chose to love her
He tried to shield himself
From the hurt and the tears
But in the end he was powerless
To stop himself from falling
He knew the risks of loving her
But still he took the chance
He knew the consequences
But still he chose to love
He warned himself not to fall again
But in the end he was helpless
In the face of true love
He fell again and again
And though he may have warned himself
His heart knew the truth

That he could never truly stay away
From the girl he loved so deeply.

35. I Warned Myself Again

Once upon a time,
I warned myself not to fall,
To love again,
With her.
Her eyes, so bright and blue,
Her smile, so sweet and true,
Her touch, so gentle and kind,
But my heart, it was on my mind.
I knew I couldn't trust her,
She had hurt me before,
But somehow, I couldn't resist,
And I fell for her once more.
Now I'm left with a broken heart,
And the pain is all too real,
But I won't make the same mistake,
I'll never love her again, I'll seal.
So to all those who think they can,
I warn you now, don't take the chance,
Love may be sweet, but it can also be cruel,
And you don't want to end up a fool.

36. You Are Fine Like Wine

He waited for her for so long,
His heart beating fast and strong.
Finally, she stood before him,
A vision of beauty, perfect and slim.
Her hair flowed like a river of gold,
Her eyes sparkled like diamonds so bold.
He felt so alive, so full of joy,
As if he'd been reborn, a new man, oh boy.
She was like wine, getting better with age,
Her presence a balm, a soothing massage.
He felt a fire burning in his soul,
Her love making him whole, making him whole.
He knew in that moment, she was his one and only,
The one he'd waited for, the one he'd been dreaming of daily.
Together, they would conquer the world,
Their love strong and true, a bond that would never unfurl.
He felt so alive, so full of life,
Seeing her after all these years, a wonderful surprise.
She was perfect like wine, getting better with time,
And he knew that together, they would be just fine.

37. Confession One

When I saw your eyes,
A fire ignited inside,
But I couldn't find the words
To express what I felt inside.
Your eyes were like stars,
Shining bright and true,
But my tongue was tied,
And I couldn't speak to you.
I wanted to tell you
Of the love that I felt,
But the words wouldn't come
And my heart just felt like it was melting.
So I stood there in silence,
Afraid to speak my mind,
Hoping that you'd somehow see
The love that I had inside.
But alas, my fear won out,
And I couldn't find the courage,
To express the feelings
That your eyes had brought to life.
But I'll never forget
The way you looked at me,

And I'll always regret
The words that I couldn't speak.

38. You Are To Be Loved Again

He wanted to tell her how he felt
His love for her burning bright
But his cruel past held him back
And filled him with self-doubt and fright
He thought he wasn't worthy of love
That he would never be good enough
His past had left him feeling broken
And the fear of rejection was tough
But still he longed to tell her
Of the love that burned within
But the fear of being rejected
Kept him silent, unable to begin
He watched her from afar
His heart heavy with despair
Afraid to take the chance
And show her how much he cared
But deep down, he knew
That he had to take the leap
To put his heart on the line
And hope that she would keep

So he gathered all his courage
And took a step forward, bold
He told her how he felt
His love for her, to be told
And to his surprise and delight
She looked at him with love in her eyes
And in that moment, he knew
That he would be loved again, no more lies.

39. 'A'ce She Is

She walks with grace,
Head held high,
A smile on her face,
A glow in her eyes.
Her confidence shines,
Bright as the sun,
She lives her life,
With joy and fun.
She doesn't shy away,
From anything she wants,
She goes after it,
With all her heart.
Her spirit is strong,
Her passion unending,
She's a force to be reckoned with,
A true queen, unyielding.
Her laughter fills the air,
Her joy contagious,
She's a light in the darkness,
A beacon, so gracious.
She's a girl of strength,
A woman of power,

MANU

She lives life to the fullest,
In every hour.
I'm lucky to know her,
To call her a friend,
Her spirit and confidence,
Are things I'll never comprehend.
She's a shining star,
A true beauty inside and out,
She's a girl who lives life,
With no fear or doubt.

40. Those Butterfly Eyes

Butterfly eyes, oh how they shine
Like twin suns that light up the sky
With their captivating gaze
They mesmerize and leave me in a daze
Your eyes are like precious gems
That sparkle and glimmer in the light
With their delicate, fluttering wings
They make my heart take flight
Butterfly eyes, oh how they glow
With a radiance that's all their own
In them I see beauty and grace
A sight that leaves me without a trace
Your eyes are like the stars above
That twinkle and dance in the night
With their captivating allure
They fill my soul with delight
Butterfly eyes, oh how they shine
You are the one that I want to make mine
With your captivating gaze
You leave me mesmerized every time.

41. On A Dream Cruise With Dreams

On a cruise ship, sailing the sea
I met a girl, oh so fine
In just two days, we spent time
Fantasies filled my mind
Of romancing her, so divine
But alas, it was all in vain
For our time together was fleeting and plain
We danced and laughed, shared stories and drinks
But in the end, it was just a fleeting fling
I'll cherish the memories we made
But now it's time for us to fade
Into the sunset, on separate paths we go
But the time we had, I'll never let it go.

42. Have Some Patience

He feels so bad inside,
When she loses patience and misunderstands him.
His heart is heavy and his mind is full of doubt,
As he tries to make things right, but she won't listen.
He knows he has to take the blame,
For letting his emotions get the best of him.
But he can't help but feel the pain,
When she rejects his apologies and turns away.
He wants to explain, to make her see,
That he never meant to hurt her or make her mad.
He only wants to love and cherish her,
But she won't give him the chance.
He feels so lost and alone,
As he tries to fix what he broke.
He hopes she will forgive him,
And let him back into her heart.
But until then, he'll keep trying,
To show her how much he cares.
For he knows that deep down inside,
She still loves him, and he still loves her.

43. Fighting Addiction

A guy once had a vice,
A habit he couldn't suffice,
He craved it day and night,
And let it consume his sight.
At first it gave him pleasure,
A momentary treasure,
But soon it turned to pain,
And caused him endless strain.
He tried to quit and break the hold,
But the addiction was far too bold,
It crept into his every thought,
And left his life fraught.
He lost his job and friends,
His health began to bend,
He hit rock bottom fast,
And his future looked aghast.
But then he found the strength,
To overcome the length,
Of his addiction's grip,
And finally took a grip.
He sought help and support,
And found a new retort,

To the demons in his mind,
And left his past behind.
Now he's on the mend,
And his future looks to trend,
Towards a brighter light,
Free from addiction's sight.

44. Breaking Through It

He wakes up every day
Feeling empty and lost
His addiction consumes him
No matter how much he tries
He can't break free
He's lost in a cycle
Of endless craving and despair
His body begs for more
But his mind knows the truth
This addiction is killing him
He's tried to quit so many times
But the pull is too strong
He's trapped in a downward spiral
And he can't see a way out
He's alone in this battle
No one can understand
The pain and the struggle
That consumes him every day
But deep down, he knows
That he's strong enough to break free
He'll fight with all his might
To break this addiction, once and for all

He'll take it one day at a time
And with every passing moment
He'll get closer to his goal
To a life of freedom and hope
He knows it won't be easy
But he's determined to win
To break this addiction
And finally be free.

45. Realisation

He felt so great being an addict
His mind was in a constant state of bliss
The rush of the drugs, the high of the drink
These were the things that made him feel alive
He didn't care about the consequences
The broken relationships, the lost opportunities
All that mattered was the next hit, the next sip
The addiction consumed him, and he reveled in it
But deep down, he knew it couldn't last
The addiction would eventually destroy him
The highs would turn to lows, the joy to pain
But for now, he embraced his addiction with reckless abandon
His friends and family tried to intervene
But he pushed them away, unwilling to change
He was too entrenched in his addiction
To even consider a life without it
But as time passed, the addiction took its toll
His health declined, his relationships suffered
He realized too late the cost of his addiction
But it was too late to turn back, he was trapped
So he continued on his downward spiral
Until finally, his addiction claimed his life

Leaving behind a trail of regret and sorrow
A cautionary tale of the dangers of addiction.

46. Fighting Anxiety

A guy once lived in fear and doubt
His anxiety would twist and shout
It ruled his mind and clouded his sight
And made it hard to face the light
But he was strong and full of grace
And he refused to give in to his fear
He fought each day and never looked back
And slowly, he began to clear
His mind of all the thoughts that weighed him down
He learned to let go and to let it be
And as he did, he found new strength
To face the world and all it could bring
He learned to breathe and to be present
To live in the moment, not in the past
And as he did, his anxiety receded
Leaving him free at last
He learned a lot along the way
About himself and how to heal
And though he still has bad days
He knows he can always find the will
To face his fears and to move on
And to live a life that is rich and true

So here's to the guy who fought with his anxiety
And learned a lot along the way too.

47. Fighting Depression

He was lost in a sea of despair,
With no light to guide him there.
His thoughts consumed by darkness,
His heart weighed down by pain.
But he fought, oh how he fought,
Against the demons in his mind.
He learned to let go of the lies,
The ones that kept him blind.
He discovered the power of self-love,
And the strength that comes from within.
He learned to forgive and to heal,
To let go and start anew.
He battled his depression day by day,
And slowly but surely he began to see the light.
His mind grew stronger, his heart more free,
As he let go of the lies and learned to be.
He is not perfect, but he is enough,
And he continues to grow and learn each day.
He has found his way out of the darkness,
And into the light of a brighter tomorrow.

48. Fighting Arrogance

Once he was a man of pride,
Full of arrogance deep inside,
He thought he knew it all,
But that was just a fall.
He fought with his ego,
And it seemed to grow,
He couldn't see the light,
And was lost in his own might.
But then he learned a lesson,
And his arrogance began to lessen,
He realized that he was wrong,
And it took some time to belong.
He started to un-learn,
And it was a tough return,
To a place of humility,
And finally, he could see.
Now he's a man of grace,
No longer stuck in his own space,
He's learned to listen and to see,
And to be the person he was meant to be.

49. Fighting Anger

Once a man consumed by anger,
Fought with his emotions every day.
His temper would flare,
And cause him much despair.
But he knew he had to change,
To rid himself of this rage.
He sought out help,
To control his inner self.
He learned to breathe and count to ten,
To pause before he let his anger win.
He practiced mindfulness,
And slowly but surely, his anger diminished.
Through therapy and introspection,
He discovered the root of his frustration.
And with time and effort,
He began to let go of his negative emotion.
He unlearnt the habits that fed his anger,
And replaced them with healthy coping strategies.
Now he is a man at peace,
No longer consumed by anger and its release.
He is grateful for the journey,
Though at times it was painful and hard.

For through it he has grown,
And learned to be in control of his own.
He is stronger, wiser, and kinder,
A better man for having fought his anger,
And unlearnt the habits that held him back,
Now moving forward with a heart full of gratitude and lack.

50. Fighting Ego

He fought with his ego
Day and night,
But in the end,
He won the fight.
He learned a lot
During the process,
Unlearning old habits
And embracing new ones.
He let go of pride
And embraced humility,
Realizing that his ego
Was only causing him anxiety.
He found a new sense of peace
And a deeper understanding
Of who he really was
And what he wanted in life.
The journey wasn't easy,
But it was worth it,
For in the end,
He emerged a better man,
Free from the chains of his ego
And ready to live life to the fullest.

51. Stillness Is The Key

He sat quietly,
In deep contemplation,
Trying to be still,
In search of the key.
The teachings of the stoic,
Guiding his way,
He sought the path to peace,
Through stillness each day.
He let go of his thoughts,
His fears and his worries,
Embracing the present,
In stillness he buries.
He found solace in silence,
In the stillness of his mind,
A sense of calm and clarity,
A world of peace he finds.
With each passing moment,
He grows stronger and bolder,
In stillness he finds power,
A strength to overcome.
He learned the true value,
Of stillness and peace,

MANU

The key to happiness,
And a life lived at ease.
So he sits, still and quiet,
In the midst of chaos and noise,
His mind at peace,
In stillness he enjoys.

52. So Far So Good

He felt so far, so good,
In a world that often misunderstood,
A place where he could be himself,
And not be judged for anything else.
He found a sense of peace and calm,
In the midst of a chaotic storm,
A place where he could breathe and think,
And not be weighed down by the heavy brink.
He felt so far, so good,
In a place where he was understood,
Where he could be who he wanted to be,
And not be hindered by society.
He found solace in the quiet moments,
In the stillness of the night,
A place where he could find his soul,
And let his spirit take flight.
He felt so far, so good,
In a world that was his own,
A place where he could be free,
And not be held back by what others see.
He found joy in the simple things,
In the beauty of the natural world,

A place where he could be at ease,
And let his heart unfurl.
He felt so far, so good,
In a world that was his own,
A place where he could be himself,
And not be defined by anyone else.

53. Your Voice Plays In My Head

He feels a flutter in his chest
Whenever she calls out his name
With her sweet and gentle voice
He can't help but feel adored
Her words are like music to his ears
They make him feel so special
So cute and full of cheer
He loves the way she says his name
It sounds like a poem in itself
A melody that fills his heart with joy
And leaves him feeling so content
He never tires of hearing her speak
For her voice is like a soothing balm
That calms his nerves and makes him weak
So whenever she calls him by his name
He knows that she truly cares
And he feels so loved and so alive
Whenever she speaks to him with her sweet voice.

54. It Hurts When You Are Not Beloved

He's lost in a sea of confusion
Feeling so alone and misunderstood
She's the one he loves
But she doesn't understand
He tries to explain himself
But the words get lost in translation
He feels like he's talking to a wall
No matter what he says, she just doesn't get it
He's tired of feeling invisible
Like he doesn't matter to her
He longs to be seen and heard
To be valued and appreciated
But she's too busy with her own world
To see the pain he's in
He's drowning in his own thoughts
As she remains oblivious to his cries for help
He's exhausted from trying
From hoping she'll finally see
That he's not just some guy
But a person with feelings and needs

So he gives up and walks away
Hoping she'll one day realize
What she's lost in not understanding him
And maybe then, they can start again.

55. Eternal Problem Of Love

He wanders the earth, a man lost and forlorn

In search of a truth that's evaded him for too long

For years he's been fighting, a never-ending war

To find the key to a love that's so much more

He's tried every method, every trick and scheme

But still he finds himself alone, trapped in a dream

He yearns for the touch of a gentle hand

To feel the warmth of a heart that understands

But how does one find love, in this cruel and cold world?

How does one become beloved, in a sea of swirling uncertainty?

He's tried to be kind, to give and to share

But still he remains alone, with nobody to care

He's tried to be strong, to hide his true self

But still he remains hidden, on a shelf

He yearns for the chance to break free from the chains

To find a love that's not just a game

But still he keeps fighting, refusing to give up

For deep down he knows that love is worth it, no matter the cost

He'll keep searching for the answer, no matter the time

For he knows that one day, he'll finally be loved and beloved, just fine.

56. Trying

He sits alone, staring at the stars
His heart is heavy, full of scars
He loves her deeply, with all his soul
But she just doesn't seem to know
He's tried to show her, time and time again
But she just doesn't seem to understand
He's laid his heart out on the line
But still, she leaves him all alone to pine
He wonders why she can't see
The love he has for her, so pure and free
He wishes she would open her eyes
And see the love that shines so bright
But still, she remains oblivious
To the love that he so willingly gives
And he feels so pathetic, so small
As she continues to ignore his call
But still, he holds on to hope
That one day she will see
The love he has for her, so true and real
And finally, she will make him whole.

57. Eye Catching You Are

A guy so eager to see her
In the morning light
Just to feel her beauty
With his whole heart
As the sun peeks over the horizon
He can't wait to catch a glimpse
Of her face, her smile
That fills his heart with joy
Her eyes sparkle like the stars
Her skin glows like the moon
Her hair flows like a river
She is his heart's delight
With every morning he awakens
He can't wait to see her again
To feel her warmth, her love
To be by her side once more
For she is the one he loves
The one he adores
The one he wants to spend
Every moment with from now until forevermore.

58. Girl With Her Swag

He was amazed, captivated
By her swag, her style
The way she moved and spoke
Had him hooked for a while
Her confidence, her grace
Was like a force to be reckoned with
She owned the room, commanded attention
And he couldn't help but admire it
Her attitude, her flair
Was something he'd never seen
She marched to the beat of her own drum
And he was in awe, so serene
He was drawn to her, enamored
By the way she held herself high
She radiated positivity
And he wanted to be by her side
She was one of a kind, unique
A force to be reckoned with
And he was grateful to have met her
The girl with swag, on her own terms.

59. Change Is Constant

Scared like shit, the guy did feel
As changes came, with no appeal
His life was turned, upside down
No longer steady, on stable ground
Once certain, now filled with doubt
He struggled to figure it out
But fear not, dear guy, you'll see
That change can bring new victory
Embrace the unknown, don't resist
For in it lies, a chance to list
New experiences, and growth within
A chance to start, a chance to begin
So take a deep breath, and hold on tight
The ride may be rough, but it'll be alright
For in the end, you'll come out strong
Ready for the next change, to which you belong

60. Just How The Life Has Turned

Once a young man, full of fear and doubt
Wary of change, he would cry and pout
But as time passed, and people changed
He realized that life was rearranged
He saw his friends grow and move on
And felt a pain that he couldn't outrun
But in his heart, he knew it was right
For them to spread their wings and take flight
He felt a shift within his soul
As he embraced the unknown
He let go of his fear and doubt
And found a new path to figure out
Now a man, no longer so young
He looks back with a smile and a pun
Grateful for the lessons he learned
As he watched others' lives turn and churn
For change may be scary, but it's a part of life
And to grow, we must embrace it with all our might
So let go of your fears, and let change set you free
And discover the person you're meant to be.

61. Ego And Pain: The Suffocation

Once a heart of gold,
Now filled with ice and cold,
A boy once full of love,
Now filled with hatred from above.
His heart once open and free,
Now closed off, unable to see,
The beauty that once was his,
Now lost in a world of selfishness.
A girl once held his heart,
But she tore it apart,
And left him broken and alone,
His trust in love forever gone.
He thought she was his everything,
But she proved to be nothing,
But a deceitful and cruel lie,
Leaving him to live a life of sighs.
His ego now inflated,
His heart no longer elated,
He walks through life with a cold stare,
His once gentle soul now filled with despair.

MANU

But even in his darkest hours,
There may still be a spark of light,
A glimmer of hope that love can heal,
And restore his heart to what it once was, real.

62. She: The Perfect Chaos

I once felt a love so strong,
For a girl with hair of burgundy.
Her eyes, like stars, shone bright,
And in them, I lost sight.
But then, I met another girl,
With hair of golden blonde.
She smiled and my heart stirred,
But something inside me hung on.
I couldn't shake the memory,
Of the girl with hair so deep.
Her touch, her kiss, her laugh,
Kept me from loving another.
Though I tried to let her go,
My heart still yearned for the one before.
I couldn't help but compare,
And in the end, I couldn't love once more.
The girl with hair of burgundy,
Had left a mark on my soul.
And though I tried to move on,
I just couldn't let her go.
So I sit here, alone and lost,
Wishing for what could have been.

MANU

But I know deep down inside,
I'll never love another girl again.

63. When Is Right Time For The Right Card

He loves with all his heart
But every time it falls apart
His trust and faith he tries to keep
But each time he takes a leap
He wants to give his everything
But ends up with a broken wing
His soul aches and his heart bleeds
As he constantly gets deceived
He cries out for help and love
But always ends up pushed and shoved
He longs for a hand to hold
But his cries are left untold
He tries to stand tall and strong
But each time he falls down and wrong
He wonders when his pain will end
And when he'll finally find a friend
He wants to give his heart to someone
But fears he'll end up all alone
So he holds back and keeps his guard
Hoping one day he'll find his card

He waits for the right one to come
And finally heal his wounds
Until then he'll keep on trying
And keep on searching for his happily ever after.

64. Deep End

With every passing day,
My heart aches more and more,
For the love I thought was true,
Has left me on the floor.
I've cried out to the heavens,
Prayed for a sign,
But no answer comes,
Only silence and time.
But I won't give up,
I'll keep faith and trust,
In the Lord above,
Who knows what is just.
For though my love may fade,
His love for me will never die,
And one day I'll find my way,
To a love that will never lie.
So I'll keep holding on,
To the hope that He provides,
And put my faith in His hands,
For the love that I desire.

65. Dandelions and Roses

Never imagined my life whole life would be this great.
Making the same mistake over and over again, staying in that
noxious feeling
Felt that it was the greatest feeling to delve into than love
But you showed me not only a dandelion can fly but a rose with
thorns as well
Soaking up the sun after waking up with a wet pillow
Trying to make sense of the shit that had happened in life
Felt that it was the best thing to do to move on
But you showed me not only dandelion is beautiful but a rose as
well with thorns.
Swelling eyes, soaring throat, sleepless nights by getting high
Thought it was the only way to escape reality
Not the other way around to accept as I am
But you showed me not only a dandelion is plucked but a rose
with thorns as well
Filling the void, trying to soothe the pain to escape from the
noxious feeling
thought that it would soothe the pain of heartbreak
Not realising that I would cause pain to them
But you showed not only dandelion is loved but roses though it
has thorns